THE FIVE-MINUTE

EYE

MAKEOVER

THE FIVE-MINUTE
EYE
MAKEOVER

CHRISTINE MOODIE

Conceived and produced by Breslich & Foss, London

Photography by Gerald Wortman
Illustrations by Marilyn Leader
Text written in collaboration with Laura Wilson
Designed by Clare Finlaison
Original design by Lisa Tai

Published by Crown Publishers, Inc., 201 East 50th Street
New York, New York 10022.
A member of the Crown Publishing Group.

CROWN is a trademark of Crown Publishers, Inc.

Manufactured in Singapore

Library of Congress Cataloging-in-Publication Data

Moodie, Christine.
The five-minute eye makeover / Christine Moodie.
p.   cm.
1. Beauty, Personal.   2. Eyes—Care and hygiene.
3. Cosmetics   I. Title.
RA778.M5715 1992
646.7'26—dc20   91–27706
                                           CIP

ISBN 0-517-58764-5

10 9 8 7 6 5 4 3 2 1

First American Edition

CONTENTS

THE FIVE-MINUTE APPROACH

Although we experiment with makeup in our teens, most of us end up with one basic look which is never varied; lack of time and confidence tend to make it impossible to change the comfortable old makeup that we could probably apply in our sleep, if necessary. Yet how much do you have stashed away – impulse buys used once and then discarded? How often do you look at a picture in a magazine and wish you could look like the model? Well, you can. Of course, makeup alone can't heighten your cheekbones or straighten your nose, but it can certainly help you achieve a cover girl look if applied correctly. Take another look at all that rejected makeup that you haven't quite had the heart to throw out. Some of those despised old eyeshadows may be the basis of a whole new look.

The makeups on the following pages are intended as guidelines only. Don't be rigid: you can take something from one look and add it to another for a different effect. Play around and discover what suits you. It takes surprisingly little practice to become a five-minute makeup artist. The most important piece of equipment is a well-lit mirror. You don't need a vast amount of equipment or a huge palette of colors. A lot of things can be put to other uses – eyeshadow can be turned into eyeliner with the aid of a wet brush, mascara can be used to darken your eyebrows as well as your lashes, and foundation or blusher can serve as eyeshadow. Don't be fooled by the range and diversity of cosmetics available – people have been painting their faces since time began, and you don't absolutely have to have the latest miracle eyeliner pen in order to achieve that special effect. It's better to keep a few reliable cosmetics than a whole range of unsatisfactory bargain items.

Mirror

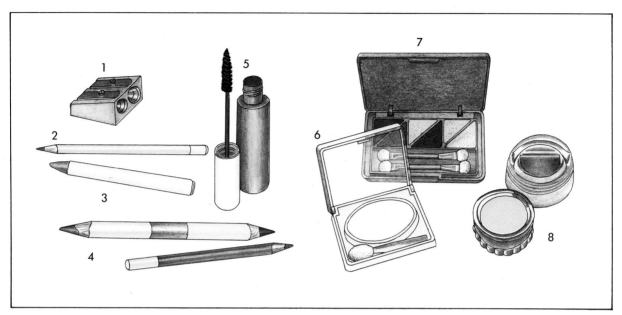

1 *Eye pencil sharpener*
2 *Eyebrow pencil*
3 *Eye crayon*
4 *Eye pencils*
5 *Mascara*
6 *Pearly powder eyeshadow*
7 *Matte powder eyeshadow*
8 *Cream eyeshadow*

EYE CARE

The eye is a delicate mechanism and the skin around it is fragile, supported by a series of muscles which are constantly being used. This results in a series of lines, and often crows' feet as well. This is a part of the natural aging process which takes place throughout the body – constant care will help to slow it down, but no amount of beauty treatments, however carefully applied, will guarantee you eternal youth. However, there's no need to help it along deliberately. Here are a few do's and don'ts:

- Always try to get a decent amount of sleep. Your body, and especially your eyes, will let you know how much you need. Fatigue invariably leads to redness around the eyes, bags and dark shadows. If your eyes are tired and dry or irritated by hay-fever, try not to rub them.

- Make time to rest your eyes for ten minutes after a busy day. Place a piece of cucumber or cotton ball dampened with witch hazel or a gentle skin tonic or astringent over each eye, lie back and simply relax. Always do this indoors or in the shade. If you lie in hot sun with damp cotton balls on your eyes, you are risking swollen eyelids.

- If you are on a long flight or train journey, take ten minutes to close your eyes and relax. Stress and worry can cause fatigue and insomnia, neither of which are any good for your eyes.

- Invest in a pair of good sunglasses. It's worth paying a little extra for a pair with nonreflective glass. Remember, you are buying eye protection as well as a fashion item. Always use them for driving on sunny days, and be sure to put on sunglasses or an eyeshade when sunbathing or sitting under an infrared lamp. Few things age the skin faster than ultraviolet rays.

- Have your eyes tested regularly. If you neglect your eyesight, you'll find yourself developing all sorts of bad habits – squinting, frowning, screwing up your eyes – in an effort to see properly.

- Don't leave your makeup on overnight.

- Remove makeup carefully. Take off your eye makeup before turning your attention to the rest of your face, so that you don't end up just scrubbing over it with a cotton ball (see page 10).

- Avoid overuse of cosmetic eye drops. Although they are useful if your eyes need freshening up (if, for example, you are tired, or your eyes have been irritated and made bloodshot by dust or wind), excessive use can lead to

Tissues

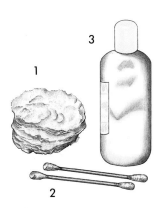

1 Cotton pads
2 Q-tips
3 Eye makeup remover

cataracts. If you want to bathe your eyes, it's better to use a medicinal eyebath. Never use cosmetic eye drops with contact lenses. If your eyes are constantly dry and sore, consult your doctor or optician.

- Don't read in a poor light, because it can give you eye strain. Try not to use your eyes excessively – sitting for long hours staring at a computer screen, or watching television or videos for very long periods can also lead to eye strain. Blink frequently – never stare. It seems absurd to have to remember to blink, but it is very important, as it gives the eye the oxygen it needs.

- Wear goggles for swimming – the chlorine in swimming pools is a known irritant, and it can leave your eyes red and stinging.

- Water retention can lead to bags under the eyes, and excessive alcohol intake is especially bad. Smoking is also unhelpful, especially as many smokers develop bad facial habits such as squinting. Try not to sit for too long in a smoky atmosphere, as this dries out the natural moisture of the eyes and can lead to redness and stinging.

- Never lend your cosmetics or eye bath to anyone. This is a sure way to spread eye infections such as conjunctivitis ("pink eye"), which can be very unpleasant.

- Why not try some eye exercises? Place your third finger below your eyebrow so that you can feel a slight pull when you close your eyes and blink rapidly, gradually moving your finger along the ridge of your eyebrow. Lift your finger up when you move it to avoid pulling at the skin or use a little eye cream. This exercise helps to stop the muscles from slackening and allowing the upper lid to droop down over the eye.

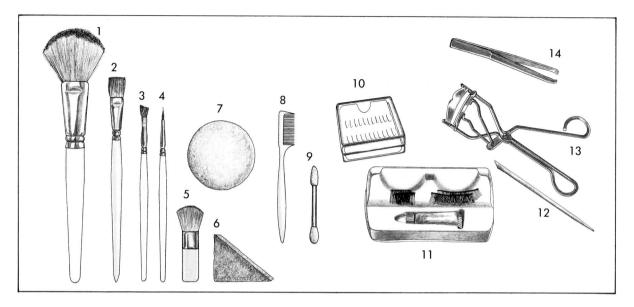

1 Big blusher brush
2 Eyeshadow brush
3 Brush with oblique bristles
4 Eyeliner brush
5 Flat blusher brush
6 Triangular sponge
applicator
7 Powder puff
8 Comb for eyebrows and
eyelashes
9 Sponge applicator
10 Individual false
eyelashes
11 False eyelash set with
glue
12 Orange stick
13 Eyelash curlers
14 Tweezers

REMOVING EYE MAKEUP

Apply your chosen cleanser to a cotton pad and wipe downwards and inwards over your closed eyelid. To remove makeup from your lower lid, wipe towards your nose. Make sure that you have not left any of the cotton behind, as wisps sticking onto your lashes may end up in your eyes, which is very uncomfortable.

Take care when choosing an eye makeup remover, as those with synthetic oils are difficult to remove and may leave a residue. Try to choose a remover with a flower oil base – blue cornflower is especially good. It should be a fine, soft liquid with a rapid cleansing action. Make sure that you have plenty of cotton pads handy; it is not a good idea to remove makeup with harsh tissues. If you have run out of cotton pads, take a piece of tissue and apply extra cleanser to make it softer and more pliable.

If you apply makeup or cleanser with your fingers, always use your third finger, which has less pressure than your first finger. This may require practice, but it will be worth it. You should never tug at the sensitive skin around the eye more than is absolutely necessary. When you massage your eyes, or apply eye creams, make a circular clockwise movement with your third finger. After cleansing, make gentle circular movements over your eyes and temples with your fingers for a soothing massage. This is especially good if you suffer from sinus problems, as these can make the area around the eyes extremely painful and give your eyes a dull, heavy look.

Use eye creams sparingly. Don't slap on a whole lot of cream before you go to sleep, as it will leave a greasy build-up on the skin – your skin stops absorbing cream after twenty minutes. Avoid thick creams or anything with a heavy lanolin base. If you do want to use a cream, choose a thin one. Like cream, oil should not be left on the eyes overnight, as it will make them puffy and there is always the risk that it will get into the corner of the eye.

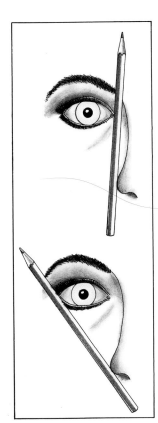

EYEBROW CARE

Pluck your eyebrows regularly to keep them in shape. To determine the natural length of your eyebrows, take a pencil and hold it vertically beside your nose. The edge of the pencil will determine the inner extent of your eyebrow. Then, keeping the pencil's base in the same position, move the top outwards across your eye until the edge is aligned with the outer corner. The tip of the pencil then determines the outer extent of your eyebrow, so do not remove hairs to make it any shorter (see diagrams). To pluck your eyebrows, follow these steps:

1 Massage the area gently with some cleanser, wiping it away with skin tonic or astringent.

1 *Liquid eyeliner*
2 *Cake eyeliner*

2 Using a cotton ball dipped in warm water, wipe over the area. The warmth of the water will enlarge the pores, making it easier to remove hairs.

3 Pull the hairs out with tweezers, plucking them as close to the roots as possible. Always pull in the direction of natural growth, and wipe away with the warm damp cotton ball as you go.

You should never pluck hairs from above the brow, and you should certainly never try to shave your eyebrows with a razor.

SOME PROBLEMS
Dark Shadows: These are usually caused by lack of sleep. If they remain after you've adjusted your sleep pattern, it could be that they are a symptom of an internal inbalance.

Bags: Both lack of sleep and fluid retention cause bags under the eyes. However, it is true that people with certain face shapes are more likely to develop bags than others – those with high cheekbones, for example, usually don't get them. Try drinking less tea and coffee, make sure you get enough early nights and rest your eyes as much as possible.

Red Eyes: Dust, wind, chlorine and tears are the main causes of red, sore eyes. Don't use cosmetic drops; bathe them with a medicinal eye bath instead, or try splashing your eyes alternately with warm and cold water.

Allergies: It is sometimes hard to establish exactly what is causing the allergy – it can even be a hypo allergenic product. Very often, the origin of your sore skin is not an allergy to a cosmetic product, which is merely the final, visible symptom of being generally tired or low. However, once you have found out what causes the allergic reaction, never use the product again – there's always the chance that the reaction might reoccur in six months' time. If you wear contact lenses, the problem may lie with the cleaning or storing fluid. It's not unknown for people suddenly to develop allergies to solutions that they've been using for years. If you are concerned, consult your optician.

Milia: These are little white fatty deposits that become trapped between the skin's layers. Don't poke at them or fiddle with them yourself – if let alone, most will disappear unaided. If you do develop a large one, have it removed by a dermatologist. If you develop any blackheads around the eye area, get these dealt with by a professional also. They can be very tricky to remove, and home methods tend to result in red gouge marks and maybe even permanent scarring.

Glasses and Contact Lenses: If you wear glasses, use a magnifying mirror when applying making up. Some types of lens distort the eye, making it look smaller. If this is the case, take a look at the tips below for small eyes. If you wear contact lenses, insert them before applying any makeup; this not only makes it easier to see, but it also means that there's no chance of mascara or powder becoming trapped painfully behind the lens. Many contact lens wearers have sensitive eyes, so choose makeup carefully – there are plenty of hypo allergenic brands available.

EYE TYPES
Here are some very general guidelines for making up different eye shapes and sizes:

Close Set Eyes: Use only pale colors on the inside of your lids, keeping the dark shadow always on the outside (see page 66).

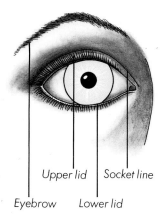

Eyebrow   Upper lid   Socket line   Lower lid

Wide Set Eyes: The socket line (see page 20) is a good look for you. Take it right into the inside corner of the eye. Dark eyeshadows are also good, as is dark eye liner taken right across to the inside corner of the eye.

Deep Set Eyes: Use pale, pastel colors and light browns (see page 30). Avoid using dark eyeshadows across the upper lid.

Small Eyes: Avoid outlining your eyes with pencil or liquid liner or applying a lot of dark shadow. Subtle shaded lines are best (see page 42).

Bulbous Eyes: Use dark shadows and eyeliners: the ideas in "Basic Brush Strokes" will be useful for you. Avoid using pearly shadows.

Droopy Eyes: When using pencils or eyeliner, always draw lines curving upwards rather than downwards. Never take a line around the outside corner of the eye, but flick the pencil upwards before you come to the turn. Lift the outer corners of your eyes with eyeshadow (see page 52).

Wrinkled Eyelids: Choose a matte shadow in preference to a pearly one, and avoid using cream shadows. Try the look on page 60.

Low Brows: Avoid using too much dark shadow or heavy eyeliner above the eye. Concentrate on the area under the eye (see page 34).

High Brows: Pluck them sparingly, not taking too much from the middle of the eyebrow. Keep the angle of the curve low – don't pluck them into a high arch. Don't apply just the one color from lashes to brow, but try dividing the upper lid into sections with different colors to make it look slightly lower (see page 74).

1
SOFT SHADES

RUSSET GLOW

What you need
Cream shadow
Applicator
Cotton pad
Matching powder
  shadow
Mascara

Warm brown shades have always been a favorite choice to compliment brown eyes, but they can look equally good with green or blue eyes. This is a perfect natural look – you can use as much or as little eyeshadow as you want. It is often a good idea to apply cream eyeshadow before powder, as it gives more depth of color and helps the powder to stay in place.

A useful tip for a neat application of powder is to hold a piece of fresh tissue paper firmly under the lower lid when applying. This prevents any falling powder from smudging your foundation. Always use a fresh cotton pad for a fresh color, or you may find you have a few more colors than you planned.

To finish this look, use a natural lip gloss and a soft honey-toned blusher. We have used a dark brown mascara here, but you can use black for extra emphasis on the lashes.

This makeup is ideal for day wear, because it is simple to apply and retouch, and it can form the basis for a dramatic evening look later.

1 *Apply cream shadow to eyelid and gently work across with applicator.*

2 *Apply powder shadow with cotton pad. Blend in.*

3 *Apply mascara.*

Colorful combinations

What you need

Three shades of powder
 shadow
Applicators
Mascara

When you are looking for a particular eyeshadow color, you often end up having to buy a pack of three colors, two of which never get used. This is a great way of utilizing them for a colorful, summer look.

We have used a combination of deep mustard, brown and lime green – not the most obvious choices, but they look stunning when put together. The basic idea of this makeup is that it goes from light to dark to light again, from just above the top lashes to the eyebrow. Whatever colors you choose, blend them well, to avoid a garish effect.

To draw the socket line, use a sponge applicator with a pointed end for clear definition. Remember that you are following the natural socket line. Before you start the makeup, close your eyes and gently run one finger across the curve of the socket to get the feel of its contours. This will help you to guide the applicator. When you draw the line under the eye, make sure that you bring the applicator right up beneath the bottom lashes, to prevent the powder smudging on your cheek. Holding a tissue firmly on the cheekbone will also help.

1 *Apply mustard eyeshadow straight across lid under socket line with applicator.*

2 *Using the brown eyeshadow, draw a line from the inside corner of the socket right across and round under the bottom lid.*

3 *Apply lime green shadow under brow and blend upwards with applicator.*

BLENDED BROWNS

What you need
Three shades of brown
  powder shadow
Sponge applicator
Mascara
Eyebrow pencil

This look is a particularly good one for large, deep-set eyes. It is a modern form of the method used by the makeup artists of 1930's Hollywood to make the eyes of the stars smoulder for the cameras, and the timeless image of Garbo's face has ensured its popularity. Here, we have used a blend of brown shades to give a more casual, outdoors effect. Try it with a dark brown mascara and a touch of brown eyebrow pencil.

When applying the darker brown, be sure to follow the natural contour of the socket. Before you start, take a good look at your eyelid in front of a well-lit mirror. You will need a firm hand and steady concentration – but if you make a mistake, don't despair. It will be easy to remove with a carefully aimed Q-tip.

To enhance this look, dust below the brow with a lighter color. Matte or very slightly pearly shadows are equally effective. Blend them in carefully to remove any hard edges.

1 *Apply khaki brown with applicator from base of top lashes, up towards natural socket line.*

2 *Apply richer brown along the line of the socket with brush, and add mascara.*

WARM ROSE

What you need
Blusher
Blusher brush
Mascara

Beauty counters always display a bewildering variety of eyeshadow colors, but it isn't necessary to have an artist's palette in order to create the look you want. This is an attractive, youthful look which requires the minimum of equipment. Any blusher can double as eyeshadow, so why not pick your favorite and apply it to your eyes as well as to your cheeks? After all, you know it suits you.

Many packs of blusher come with a flat, wide brush, which is an ideal tool for applying blusher to the eyelid. Work upwards to the brow from the middle; don't take it out sideways. Avoid putting any blusher directly under the eye, as most blushers have a pinkish tinge which could make your eyes look red-rimmed. Placing a tissue under the eye will help to prevent falling blusher from smudging on the face.

This is a useful, basic makeup – excellent for work, because it doesn't necessitate an enormous repair kit. It can easily be enhanced if you want to make a change (see page 26).

1 *Using a brush, take blusher across upper lid: work upwards to the brow from the middle of the lid.*

2 *Using the same blusher, apply a small amount to the cheek and blend in well.*

3 *Apply brown or black mascara.*

SIMPLE SOPHISTICATION

What you need
Powder shadow
Thin brush
Eyebrow pencil
Eyebrow comb

This makeup is perfect if you need to make a quick change – a business lunch, an evening out after a long day, or a frantic half-hour before the dinner guests arrive. All you need to convert the makeup on page 24 into something sophisticated is add a matching eyeshadow.

For this look, use shadow as eyeliner rather than applying it all over the surface of the lid. We have used a soft brown to blend with the rosy tone of the blusher. Use a thin brush to get a delicate line across the base of the lashes. If you want to enhance the Warm Rose look but have no eyeshadow, you can draw the line using the blusher – provided it is not too pink, as this will make your eyes look red.

When you use the eyebrow pencil, color the hairs rather than trying to make an artificial line across them. Smooth them with your finger tips for a well-defined shape or comb them with an eyebrow comb.

1 *Using a wet brush and powder eyeshadow, draw a line along the base of the top lashes.*

2 *Use brown pencil on eyebrows.*

GREEN SHADES

What you need
Three shades of green
  powder shadow
Sponge applicator
Brush
Mascara

This makeup has a three color effect – dark, lighter, lightest. Always apply the palest color first, as it is much easier and less messy than trying to blend it in at the end. Hold a tissue under the eye to prevent smudges, especially if you decide to take the green shadow underneath the eye. This gives a nice finish to the look, but it is best avoided if your eyes tend to droop at the corners. Don't use the same applicator for all the shades, or you may end up with a uniform green color instead of three subtly blended ones.

Here, the darkest color is an emerald green, but any dark shade such as a bottle green or a deep, leafy green will do. Choose the color which suits your complexion and matches your clothes. Use a brown, or black / brown mascara.

We have teamed this look with a soft shirt and ethnic jewelry to create a casual look, but it would go equally well with a party outfit or evening gown.

1 *Apply pale green over whole upper lid to brow with applicator.*

2 *Apply darker green to upper lid, blending upwards to pale green.*

3 *Add deeper green above lashes and blend.*

4 *Apply deeper green under eye with wet brush.*

SUN TONES

What you need
Pearl powder
  shadow
Matte powder
  shadow
Sponge applicator
Mascara

Pearlized eye shadows don't have to be saved for the evenings only – they can look natural as well as glamorous. This is a great look for a sunny day. Try it with a natural lipstick, and warm-toned foundation and a camisole.

Here, we have used a very pearly peach shadow on the lid and a smooth, cocoa brown just below the brow. Usually, the darker color is worn on the lid and the lighter under the brow, but in this case the colors have been used "upside down". This is especially effective if you have deep set eyes. However, it is probably one to avoid if your eyelids are wrinkled, as it does tend to highlight them.

For this look, we have used colorless mascara, which is excellent for dark lashes and can also be used for eyebrows. If your lashes are light, you may find it more convenient to have them dyed professionally – especially before your summer vacation, as the dye does not run after swimming, so you won't have to fiddle about with tissues and mascara on the beach.

1 *Apply pearl eyeshadow to upper lid with applicator.*

2 *Apply darker color under brow with applicator. Blend.*

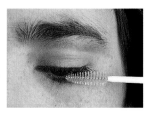

3 *Apply mascara.*

NATURAL BEAUTY

What you need
Two shades of powder
  shadow
Applicator
Thin brush
Mascara

Enhance your eyes with subtle skin tones to achieve the perfect makeup – one which doesn't seem to be there at all! Choose light beige and buff colors to match your skin tone, and use a very small amount. Use a touch of flat color for blusher and spread it evenly. If your eye lashes and brows are naturally very dark, use black mascara and eyebrow pencil. Otherwise, use a warm brown.

Smudging a small amount of beige or brown under the eyes will add depth to the lashes – but don't use too much! A dark smudged line here can look like a dark shadow under the eye.

To apply the brown shadow along the line of the lashes, use a thin brush, carefully wetted. Make sure any excess water is wiped off – the brush should be damp, not dripping. Dabble your wet brush in the powder carefully to avoid ending up with a great muddy-looking patch in the middle. You will need a steady hand to apply this eyeshadow, and it will take practice. If you don't feel confident, you can omit this step the first time.

1 *Apply natural shade to eyelid with applicator.*

2 *Put a tiny touch of light brown above the socket line and blend well.*

3 *Using an applicator smudge a small amount of beige or brown under the lower eye lashes.*

4 *Using a wet brush, put a touch of brown powder along the base of the top lashes.*

UPSIDE DOWN MAKEUP

What you need
Pale powder shadow
Eye pencil
Matching powder
  shadow
Brush

Eyeshadow is not just for the upper eyelid. It can be used just as effectively on the lower lid for this striking look. Use a light eyeshadow on the upper lid – we have used cream, but any very pale shade would be suitable – and save your darker colors for the lower lid. When you draw the pencil line below the lashes, keep the point of the pencil against them to create a slightly faded effect with the side of the tip.

We have used a bluish-gray pencil here. Charcoal gray or brown would be equally effective, but beware of anything darker, as it will tend to give a bottom-heavy look and may make the skin under the eyes appear discolored. A darker powder may not be so easy to blend in as this bluish-gray color. It is very difficult to remove makeup from directly under the lower lashes, and any scrubbing or pulling at the lower lid is best avoided. Again, using a tissue under the eye will prevent smudging. If you are worried about this step, it can be omitted. However, adding powder gives the pencil line more intensity and makes it last longer.

1 *Apply cream colored eyeshadow over upper lid, working up to eyebrow with applicator.*

2 *Draw a line under the eye with pencil.*

3 *Add powder of matching color and blend with brush.*

2
BASIC BRUSH
STROKES

INCOGNITO

What you need
Brown eye pencil
Brush
Buff powder shadow
Sponge applicator
Eyebrow comb

It takes a bit of practice to become really proficient with eyeliner, so why not try this look first?
It doesn't matter if you can't yet draw a straight line for this makeup, as smudging it upwards with the brush will remove any wobbly bits.

Instead of these natural brown colors you can use a black pencil with a gray powder, or even a navy pencil with a pale blue powder. Experiment to find out what suits you best. When you apply the powder under the brow, follow its contour – it has a natural curve that you can follow with the applicator.

Darkening your eyebrows and altering their shape can change your whole look, so this is very adaptable: it's equally effective with a trenchcoat, a Hermes scarf and pearls, or your sloppiest sweater. As long as your eyebrows are tidy and well maintained, it is easy to change the curvature, provided you always comb them in the direction of their natural growth.

1 *Draw a line with brown pencil above the top lashes.*

2 *Smudge the line upwards with brush.*

3 *Apply buff powder shadow under brow with applicator.*

4 *Darken eyebrows with pencil and comb into shape.*

MIDNIGHT BLUE

What you need
Blue cake liner
Thin brush
Mascara

This deep dark blue sets off any eye color and complexion beautifully. Here, it it dressed down with denim for a casual, sporty feel, but this striking color can equally well be used for an evening look.

For this simple makeup, you need either a cake eyeliner with a brush, as shown here, or a liquid eyeliner. If you are using cake liner, mix it carefully with water, using a brush. Never wet the eyeliner directly from the tap. It is better to have a small bowl of water on your dressing table. Keep the bowl filled with clean water and rinse brushes after use to prevent the bristles becoming clogged with old makeup.

For this line, choose a thin brush. If you want to thicken up the line, draw a base line right along the top of the lashes first, for guidance, and then build on it with separate brush strokes.

Use a black mascara for this look, as it is better to have a strong, darker color than an imperfect match of blues. Although blue and purple mascaras can look striking, they tend to end up looking simply bizarre, so are best avoided.

1 *Mix eyeliner using a thin wet brush.*

2 *Apply liner across upper lid with brush.*

DOE-EYED BEAUTY

What you need

Bottle-green powder
  shadow
Light brown cake liner
Brush
Sponge applicator
Mascara

This beautiful makeup, popularized by Audrey Hepburn in the 1950s, still looks as good today. Intensely stylish, it looks best with a Chanel-type suit, delicate jewelry and gloves for a thoroughly well-groomed air.

This is slightly more difficult than a basic socket line or line along the base of the top lashes, so it may take some practice. For this look, eyeshadow has been wetted and used as eyeliner. The half socket line should be very subtle, so apply it lightly. If it goes wrong, don't panic – you can always do a full socket line and turn it into something else.

The small smudge of brown powder under the eye will help to make it look larger – but it must be just a small touch of makeup, on the very outer edge of the lower lid. Use a brown or black mascara and matching eyebrow pencil. Brush your eyebrows into a neat line – if there are any straggling hairs which refuse to stay in place, remove them with tweezers.

1 *Apply bottle-green powder shadow in a thick line along base of top lashes, using a wet brush.*

2 *Lightly brush in a half socket line using the same color, and blend.*

3 *Mix light brown cake liner with water, and paint a thin line on top of the thick one.*

4 *With the sponge applicator, add a touch of brown powder under the outer corner of the eye.*

FALSE EYELASHES

What you need
False eyelashes
Eyelash glue
Tweezers
Orange stick
Eyeliner
Thin brush

Although the popularity of false lashes has declined in recent years, there was a time when a lot of women wouldn't leave home without them. Nowadays, false lashes come in all shapes and sizes. You can trim them to any length and use as many or as few as you like.

This look is for a full set of upper lashes. They are always the last thing to add to a makeup; put everything else on beforehand. Paint on a thin black line just above the natural lashes beforehand, so that there is no telltale gap (see page 46).

Be careful when applying the special glue which comes with the lashes. Never use any other type of glue. Always use an orange stick, never use your finger. It is easy to smear glue, and if it is left on the lashes, it will dry white: it dries clear on the eyelid itself. You can adjust the lie of the lashes while it is drying – when you blink, it will be obvious where the lashes are likely to come off, so make sure you press down firmly on those areas. Push lashes upwards from underneath with the side of your finger to check that the glue is dry.

1 *After drawing a thin black line above the top lashes, pick up eyelash firmly in the middle with tweezers. Apply glue with orange stick.*

2 *Still holding lash in tweezers, apply to center of upper eyelid. Adjust position.*

3 *Press lashes firmly into place with orange stick or end of tweezers.*

DEEP DARK EYES

What you need
Eye pencil
Mascara
Eyelash comb
Eyebrow pencil

For this sultry look you can either use your own lashes, or false ones. Remember, if you are using false lashes, the line must be absolutely right so that there is no gap between your own lashes and the artificial ones. If you have no false lashes, then this is an opportunity to go to town with the mascara. If you have pale eyebrows, darken them up with an eyebrow pencil to balance this look.

It is easier to draw the line above the lashes in two sections: begin in the middle and follow the line of your lashes to the outer corner, where you should bring the pencil away from the natural contour of the eye in a slight upturn. When you draw the line around the inner corner of the eye, make sure it stays on the surface of the skin so that the liquidity of the eye does not cause it to clog together into a nasty little black ball.

This look can either be achieved with a soft, sharp pencil or with a cake liner and a thin brush. Some liquid eyeliners come with a brush attached, but they are often too thick for use. Thin artist's brushes are very good for this purpose.

1 *Draw a thin line with eye pencil along the base of the lashes, with a slight upturn at the outer corner.*

2 *Take the line on towards the nose, bringing it to the inner corner of the eye, down and round along the lower lid about half an inch.*

QUICK COVER-UP

What you need
Foundation
Triangular applicator
Loose powder
Blusher brush
Mascara

This makeup is useful for those days when you have no time to spare for anything elaborate. If you are dashing out to an appointment, or it's the morning after a party and you aren't feeling quite your best, this is the ideal solution. All you need are foundation, powder and mascara. Simply extend your foundation to cover your eyelids, and then apply powder to them as you do to the rest of your face with a blusher-type flat brush. Apply plenty of powder to avoid any creases forming on your eyelid. If some of the powder attaches itself to the eyelashes, you needn't wipe it off, as it will help to make them look thicker when you apply the mascara. However, if you have any lines or creases underneath your eyes, do brush this off before it gets a chance to settle and form unsightly lines.

Before you apply the mascara wand to your eyebrows, make sure that any excess is wiped off on the rim of the tube. It may be better to use a fairly old mascara for this, as there is a danger that thick, new mascara will form into lumps. If your lashes and brows are dark, try using a colorless mascara.

1 *Apply foundation across upper lid with triangular applicator.*

2 *Apply powder over lid with blusher brush.*

3 *Apply mascara, and then use wand to tidy and darken eyebrows.*

WILD CHILD

What you need
Black kohl pencil
Black matte powder
  shadow
Sponge applicator

Very urban and very tough, this look goes naturally with your leather jacket and jeans.

Kohl pencils are very soft, so you will need to sharpen it a couple of times to ensure a firm line. When you open your eye after drawing the line on the upper lid, you may find you have an additional line half way up the lid where the kohl has rubbed off. If you have, don't try to remove it but use it as a demarcation line for the powder shadow. When you are drawing a line along the lower lid, it helps to look upwards. Apply the powder shadow with a tissue held under the eye, to prevent it falling on the face. Don't be tempted to smudge the powder too much, especially under the eye, or you will be left with a ringed, panda effect.

If you have small eyes, it is best to avoid this look: a thick outline in any dark color will make them look smaller. Also, if you are prone to any discoloring or dark shadows under the eyes, this will highlight them, so use the kohl pencil sparingly. Whatever your eye shape, don't put makeup inside your eyelid as this can cause irritation.

1 *Using a black kohl pencil, draw a thick line across upper lid, and then round and down along lower lid.*

2 *Smudge slightly above and below with black matte powder, using pointed sponge applicator.*

BIG BROWN EYES

What you need
Brown eye pencil
Brown mascara

For this attractive, gentle look, it is important to be able to draw a straight line across the base of the top lashes. To keep your hand steady, try resting your elbow on the dressing table. One way of ensuring a straight line is to place your little finger on the inside corner of your upper lid, as shown here. Another method is to "stretch" the eyelid slightly by placing the little finger of your working hand at the outer corner of the eye. Don't try to get a perfect line in one go – it is far easier to make a number of shorter strokes across the lid. Make sure that the little upward flicks are at the same angle on both sides, so that you don't look lopsided. If you do make a mistake, wipe it off with a moistened Q-tip.

Use a soft pencil which won't pull at your skin. However good your pencil, these lines do tend to rub off over the course of the day so take it with you for a repair session.

When you put mascara on lower lashes, apply it with tip of wand, not with the side. If you brush at your lashes as if brushing teeth, you are likely to get blobs of mascara on the skin.

1 *Using eye pencil, draw a thin line directly above top lashes, flicking pencil upwards and outwards at outside corner.*

2 *Apply mascara to eyelashes and use to darken eyebrows.*

3
CLASSIC
COLORS

Inca Gold

What you need
Gold eye pencil
Gold powder shadow
Orange powder shadow
Rust powder shadow
Big brush
Thin brush
Sponge applicator
Mascara

This exotic golden look is especially stunning on dark skin. If you have a pale complexion, or freckles, apply a thick coat of a darker foundation to offset the eye makeup more effectively. This is definitely a bold, party look, and it won't work if you are timid with your makeup. If you really want to catch the light, you can always add a darker color under the eye for contrast and extra sparkle under the brows when you finish the makeup. Glitter makeup does have a tendancy to drift – brushing it onto a thick foundation or eyeshadow will help to anchor it. Don't worry too much if some of the initial coat of gold powder falls onto your face as it will blend in with your foundation to good effect.

Find powder shadows in complementary colors: most shades of orange and rusty brown are suitable. The colors should always be warmer and darker than the gold itself: yellowish shades will not be as effective.

Use a gold face powder, highlighting the cheekbones with broad brush-strokes.

1 *Apply gold pencil to the lid under the socket. Flick upwards slightly at outer corners.*

2 *Apply gold powder over whole eyelid with a big brush.*

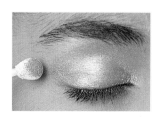

3 *Apply orange powder shadow to the outer side of the upper lid with a sponge applicator.*

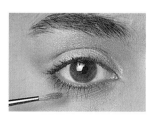

4 *Use rust colored powder shadow and a thin brush to make a line under the eye.*

PEARLY PINK

What you need
Pearly pink eyeshadow
Matte powder shadow
Sponge applicator
Thin brush
Mascara

A combination of pearl and matte eyeshadow makes a delightful evening look. We have used a pearly pink with a matte maroon color here, but any flattering combination of light and dark colors will work well. To balance your makeup, use a lipstick that matches the darker color and helps to bring up the pearly shade. Pearls are the obvious accessory here, but simple glass or crystal jewelry could be just as effective.

Use a black or brown mascara, and take care not to leave smudges when applying it to your lower lashes – it will be impossible to blot out, and you won't be able to remove it without wiping off the dark powder under the eye. Remove any smudges with the end of a Q-tip dipped in a very small amount of water or makeup remover. Use the tip of the mascara wand – this also makes it easier to separate lashes which have become stuck together. This method gives you more control over the amount of mascara you use, so try it on your top lashes as well.

1 *Apply pearly pink shadow with sponge applicator across upper lid.*

2 *Use a brush to apply a darker, matte powder shadow to the outside corner of the upper lid.*

3 *With the brush, bring the color round and under the eye, about half way across.*

PINK AND GRAY

What you need
Gray powder shadow
Pearly pink powder
  shadow
Sponge applicator
Blusher brush
Thin brush

This attractive look is suitable for all ages and skin types. It is especially good if you want something a little different to attend a formal function, such as a wedding. Accessorize with a matching pink hat, earrings and lipstick as shown here, or you could use it to brighten up a dashing all-black outfit.

This bluish-gray powder sets off blue or gray eyes beautifully, and it blurs any lines or wrinkles to create a soft, fresh look. Always place a tissue under the eye when applying the powder to prevent it from dropping on to the face – too much gray under the eyes can make them look discolored or even bruised. Choose the gray color carefully – a bluish, gunmetal gray is preferable to iron gray. For an evening effect, try a more silvery tone.

For the pink, you can use either pearly or matte eyeshadow. Use the pink to surround and offset the gray, blending the gray upwards. Apply the pink to the outer corner of the eye, rather than straight along beneath the brow. Apply the gray powder along the base of the top lashes, wetting the brush to intensify the color.

1 *Apply gray shadow to upper lid with sponge applicator.*

2 *Dust slightly pearly pink eyeshadow under brow with blusher brush.*

3 *Wet thin brush in clean water.*

4 *Apply gray shadow with wet brush above top lashes and bring round under the eye about a quarter of an inch.*

COLORFUL COPPER TONES

What you need
Matte powder
  shadow
Cotton ball
Eyeshadow brush
Eyeliner brush
Mascara
Eyelash comb
Eyebrow pencil

This rich chocolate brown makes a fabulous evening look, whatever your skin tone. It only takes one color – just use the eyeshadow as an eyeliner.

Dark colors should be applied with caution – the darker the color, the harder it is to rectify a mistake, especially if you are in a hurry. After applying, blend the eyeshadow around the outside of the eyelid and taper it off carefully. Take care not to go below the corner of the eye, as this will give a droopy effect, and it will look very peculiar if the eyeshadow comes down lower than the eyeliner. This is one case where it is essential to use a tissue to prevent smudging.

Eyeliner gives the eye more intensity and stronger definition. Don't be tempted to make the line too thin, but do taper it off at the outer corner to give it a bit of lift. Use plenty of mascara, but take care not to let it get clogged up, as this will make the lashes stick together: an eyelash comb is a vital piece of equipment.

When darkening the eyebrows, always follow the natural line of growth. Keep your eyebrow pencil sharp, in order to avoid smudging.

1 *Apply powder shadow using cotton ball. Blend with brush.*

2 *Wet the eyeshadow and apply with brush as eyeliner. Add mascara.*

3 *Comb eyebrows into shape. Darken with pencil.*

SUNBURST

What you need

Yellow powder
  shadow
Orange powder shadow
Rusty-orange powder
  shadow
Two medium-width
  shadow brushes
Blusher brush
Thin brush

This warm, summery look is especially good for pale skin. Find a combination of yellow, orange and rust colors to suit your complexion – it doesn't matter if you don't tan, because this makeup is all the more striking against a light background.

Apply the lightest color first, brushing it over the whole upper lid. This may be messy, so use a tissue to stop falling powder.

For the line under the eye, use a very small amount of powder, and make sure the tip of your brush is thin. This is just a thin line to balance the makeup and deepen the lower lashes, so you need a strong light and a steady hand. It may help to balance your elbow or even the heel of your hand on a firm surface and to use your little finger to pull the eyelid down and outwards slightly (just enough to keep the surface of the skin taut – not enough to make you look like a bloodhound).

For your blusher, either use the rust colored eyeshadow on your face, or choose a shade that blends with it.

1 *Apply yellow powder shadow over whole upper lid with brush.*

2 *Use a thin brush to apply orange shadow to outer half of socket. Then apply below brow on inside.*

3 *Apply rusty-orange shadow underneath the eye with thin brush.*

4 *Apply blusher, using large brush. Work upwards to outer edge of brow.*

CONTRASTING COLORS

What you need
Thick eye pencil
Brush
Pearly eye pencil
Pearly powder shadow

If you have a lot of makeup lying around unused, don't throw it away – it may give you a new look. For this makeup we have used a thick jade eye pencil, a pearly grape-colored pencil and matching powder shadow – hardly the most obvious combination. You can have a lot of fun picking out the least likely twosomes from your makeup box, and you'll be pleasantly surprised by the results. To get the full effect, choose a lipstick which contrasts – or even clashes – with your eye makeup, and use brightly colored accessories such as these long turquoise gloves and sparkling jet bracelet.

The most important thing to remember about this makeup is that the inside of the upper lid is light and the outside dark. For this reason, it is especially recommended for those with close-set eyes. When you draw the pencil line under your eye, start thin on the inside corner and thicken it up as you go. To get the line as close to your eye as possible, bring the tip of the pencil right up under the bottom lashes, so that you are holding it almost vertically against your cheek.

1 *Draw thick pencil line under the eye.*

2 *Blend outer edge of line with brush.*

3 *Draw short lines on outer corner below brow with pearly pencil and blend in with your finger.*

4 *Brush matching pearly powder over top lid, working your way outwards.*

IMPERIAL PURPLE

What you need
Two colors of purple
  powder shadow
Pearly purple shadow
Sponge applicator
Thin brush

This rich, strong makeup is just right for the
Christmas season. Apply the colors lavishly and
don't clutter the look with fussy jewelry or clothes.
Go for something simple, sweeping and elegant.

One word of warning before you start: for makeup
artists, as for painters, purple is a problem. It is hard
to blend, hard to mix, doesn't stick to anything and
wears off in a shorter space of time than any other
color. When you use the powder shadow, wet it or
use it over a purple colored cream shadow – either
way, there's more chance that it will stay put.
You will probably need to retouch your makeup
after you've completed the steps, because what was
a deep, lustrous purple when wet may become a
rather dismal mauve color when dry. Keep your eye
closed while the makeup is drying and always wait
until it is dry before retouching.

Hold a tissue under the eye when you apply pale
lilac powder to the upper lid because it will fall onto
your face. For the last step, use a very pearly
shadow. If you're feeling confident, try to blend it a
little, but be careful – you may end up losing the lot.

1 *Lightly dust pale lilac
powder shadow over the
whole upper lid to brow with
sponge applicator.*

2 *Using a wet brush, draw a
thick line with purple powder
shadow on upper lid.*

3 *Using pearly shadow,
make an arc directly below
the brow leaving some pale
lilac showing at outer corner.*

OLD-FASHIONED ELEGANCE

What you need

Sage green powder
  shadow
Sponge applicators
Mascara
Eyebrow pencil

Makeup in the 1920s was not as sophisticated as it is now. However, pictures of the society beauties and stars of the period show how they achieved this wonderfully languid look with the crude range of materials then available. With modern techniques and eyeshadows, it looks even better – you could try it with a cloche hat and a draped chiffon scarf like the one shown here or dress it up with a cocktail outfit.

Apply the shadow in stages – use a large amount and keep adding until you are satisfied. It can be any color, but try to avoid colors such as maroon which will look like bruises when blended under the eye. Blend carefully, so that you don't end up with a great lake of powder around each eye. If you have bags or lines under the eye, it's best not to have too much shadow on the lower lid, as the powder will highlight blemishes rather than camouflage them.

Use plenty of mascara and, if you have naturally long lashes, it might be nice to curl them with eyelash curlers. After applying eyebrow pencil, use your fingers or a comb to smooth your brows into a gentle arch for the full "period" effect.

1 Using applicator, dust sage green matte shadow onto upper eyelid.

2 Blend it upwards to the eyebrow with sponge applicator.

3 Continue blending right around eye, curving it round to lower lid.

Venetian red

What you need
Red crayon
Red powder shadow
Brown powder shadow
Pink powder shadow
Cotton pad
Brush

This sophisticated look relies on a finely judged application of crayon and powder. Too little makeup will look ineffective; too much will look overdone. It will suit any complexion, but choose the shade carefully to match your clothes and jewelry. Heavy gold earrings like those shown here work particularly well and, if your hair is long enough, sweep it well away from your face to make the most of your dazzling eyes. Balance the makeup with a bright red lipstick, but use a more muted shade for your blusher with a matte foundation.

If it is hard to obtain eye crayons, you can use non-toxic children's crayons or a red lip pencil. Powder over the crayon as you would powder over your foundation, but make sure that the cotton doesn't stick to your eyelid or attach itself to your eyelashes. For highlighter, you could use a small amount of pink or silver.

1 *Apply red crayon to upper lid and blend upwards with finger.*

2 *Apply red powder shadow to upper lid with cotton pad.*

3 *Apply a small amount of brown shadow underneath eye with wet brush.*

BLUE NOTES

What you need
Three shades of blue
  powder shadow
Brush
Sponge applicators

Wistful, mysterious, dazzling, demure, electric – blue eyeshadow is the most popular color because it can be used to create so many different looks. For this soft, almost dreamy look, we have used three shades: navy blue, gray-blue, and a delicate baby blue. There are hundreds of shades available, so mix and match to discover what you like best.

This is a subtle makeup, so apply the colors carefully, making sure they don't overspill their territories. Bring the navy blue right down to the base of the lashes in order not to leave a line showing; it won't be difficult if you use a thin brush. The gray-blue should be applied under the brow, working towards the outside edge. When you apply this, make sure that the two shades are kept separate: there should be a space between them for the pale blue color. Dust this on lightly with an applicator and blend to smooth out any hard edges.

Be wary of using blue mascara with this look as it might add a new and rather jarring element. A dark brown like the one used here blends well with the soft brown used for the eyebrows.

1 *Apply navy blue powder shadow up to socket area with brush.*

2 *Lightly color under brows in paler shade with applicator, leaving space above the dark blue.*

3 *Apply pale blue from inside corner across middle of lid.*

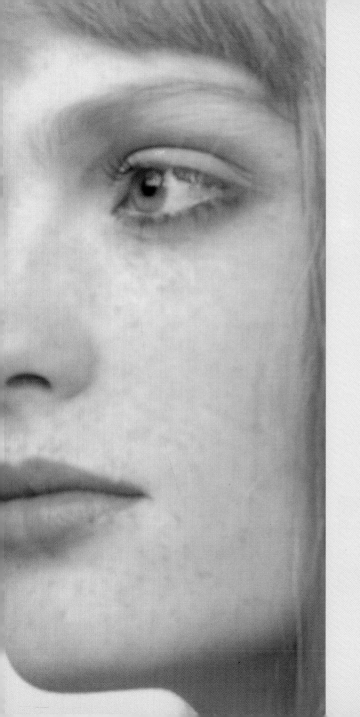

4
FANTASY

SPIDERWOMAN

What you need
Blue eye pencil
Silver eye pencil
Silver glitter powder
Sponge applicator

Trick or treat? Perfect for a Halloween party or a costume ball, this weird and wonderful look is surprisingly easy to achieve. Draw a light outline for the web first. Don't worry if you can't achieve perfect symmetry – a lop sided web is much more fun. Use different pencils (thick and thin) for the different strands. You can use either dark blue or black. The silver pencil and powder will give the web a dewy effect. If you don't possess a silver eye pencil or crayon, mix a pearly silver powder with a little water and apply it with a brush. Work carefully over the lines you have already drawn – it's important to keep the two colors distinct and unsmudged.

It's a good idea to apply the glitter powder over some sort of base; either foundation or an appropriately colored cream eyeshadow would work. Use a dark pencil to outline your eyes if you wish (see page 50 for details). This is one occasion when spider's legs are appropriate, so use as much mascara as you can stand. For a truly gothic touch, add black lipstick.

1 *Draw in the spider's web in blue pencil across the face, starting at the bridge of the nose and working outwards.*

2 *Using a silver pencil, "shadow" the lines of the web.*

3 *Using a silver glitter powder and sponge applicator, go over the lines for emphasis.*

4 *Apply the silver glitter over the entire upper lid and work up towards brow with sponge applicator.*

CAT'S EYES

What you need
Bronze pearly
  eyeshadow
Black cake liner
Sponge applicator
Thin brush
Mascara
Half lashes
Eyelash glue
Tweezers
Orange stick

If you want something thoroughly flattering for a special party, try this sleek, feline look.

Choose a pearly bronze shadow and apply it with the edge of the sponge applicator to get the angle right. Take it up and out beyond the line of your eyebrows. For catlike cheeks, use a bronze blusher and blend it upwards into the eyeshadow.

If you have pale lashes, use plenty of black mascara. You don't have to use false lashes, but if you decide to, remember to paint a black line across the base of your own before you apply them.
You can buy sets of half-lashes (the outer half), or, better still, buy a whole roll of lashes and cut off as much as you want. For a true cat effect, the outer lashes should be considerably longer than the inner ones, so taper them accordingly.

Use mascara to darken your eyebrows, but make sure there is no excess mascara on the wand before you start. Comb your brows upwards with the wand for an elegant curve. By the time you've finished, you'll be able to hear yourself purr.

1 *Apply pearly bronze eyeshadow to the upper lid, working right into inside corner and outside beyond the line of the eyebrow.*

2 *Apply black cake liner with a thin wet brush across the base of the lashes, turning down towards nose and upwards on the outside.*

3 *Apply half lashes with tweezers (see page 44).*

BUTTERFLY

For this beautiful butterfly, we have used a maroon pencil and a pearly bronze eyeshadow, but there are many other possibilities.

The most difficult part of this makeup is getting the butterfly's wings symmetrical. You need total concentration, good lighting and a steady hand. Use your eyebrows as a guideline for the top of the wings – one eyebrow is always fractionally higher than the other, so always start with that one. The antennae are optional, but if you decide to add them, they should be at a 45 degree angle from the wings. Don't do them upright, because they will look like frown lines.

Make sure the point of your pencil is kept sharp for a clear, strong outline, and avoid going over it when you color in the wings with pearly powder. Test your pencils on the back of your hand to find the most suitable and reject any that have to be pressed down hard on your skin. Always use pearly shadow for the wing color, because it is easier to blend and the butterfly will be most effective if the color is subtly varied, like the one shown here.

1 *Draw the outline, including the antennae and circles inside the wings, with an eye pencil.*

2 *Using a brush, fill in with a pearly powder shadow, leaving circles unpainted.*

3 *Use a lighter color to fill in the circles and go over the antennae (if desired).*

BLACK AND WHITE

What you need
White matte powder
  eyeshadow
Dark brown matte
  powder
Brush
Sponge applicator
Black eyeliner
False eyelashes
Eyelash glue
Tweezers
Orange stick

This look epitomizes the 1960s: Mary Quant's distinctive black and white, Twiggy's huge eyelashes, and pale, pale lipstick. Here, we have added top and bottom false eyelashes, but you can do a scaled down version for everyday wear.

Always use a matte white powder, as pearly white tends to make the eyes look bulbous. Wet the brush to give the white more density. The socket line should follow the natural curve of your socket. You can do this in either dark brown, or in black if you want a starker contrast.

Apply mascara before putting on false eyelashes, and always apply the bottom lashes last. For these bottom lashes, we have added in individual false ones. Pick up the lash in your tweezers, and dip the very tip into the glue. If you squeeze out a small amount of glue onto a flat surface, you will have more control over where it ends up; after all, you only need a touch of glue. Apply the lash to the outer corner of the lower lid with the tweezers. Move inwards, shortening the lashes as you go.

1 *Apply white matte powder shadow across lid with sponge applicator.*

2 *Paint in socket line in dark brown with brush.*

3 *Apply black eyeliner along the top of the lashes with brush.*

4 *Apply lashes (see above and page 44).*

DAISIES

What you need
White liquid liner
Eye pencil

This design is simple and eye-catching and you don't have to be a great painter to make it work. First, think about positioning and size: you could have a single large flower on one cheekbone, or a number of small ones scattered around the corner of one eye.

You can paint long thin petals like those shown here by pressing the brush flat down on the cheek, or you can simply make a ring of dots. Experiment on your hand to find the best brush for the petal shape. Remember to leave room for the center, which can be painted in any dark color. Real daisies, of course, have yellow centers, but yellow will not show up unless you paint a big flower. We have used bottle green here, but black, brown or dark blue will be equally effective.

If you can't get hold of a white liquid liner, you can use white powder shadow or cake liner, mixing with water until you achieve the proper consistency.

Small green leaves can be applied using green powder shadow and the flat of a wet brush, or you can place your daisies against a "lawn" of green eye makeup (see page 76).

1 *Paint a ring of petals with white liquid liner, leaving a space for the center.*

2 *Using a sharp eye pencil, put a dot in the center of the petals.*

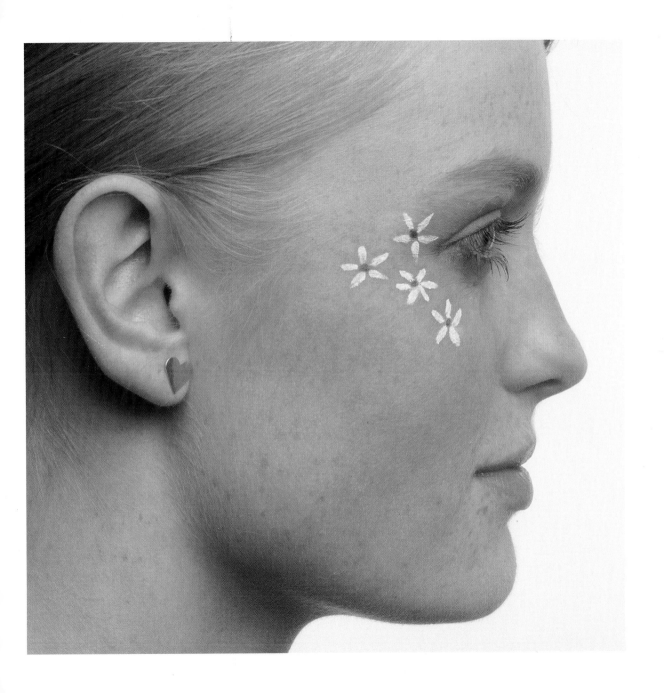

INDEX